This Wedding Planner Belongs To:

_____

Initial Planning Phase

IDEAS FOR THEME

IDEAS FOR VENUE

IDEAS FOR COLORS

IDEAS FOR MUSIC

IDEAS FOR RECEPTION

OTHER IDEAS

Notes & Ideas

Wedding Budget Planner

Expense MANAGER

CATEGORY/ITEMS	BUDGET	ACTUAL COST	BALANCE

Wedding Budget Checklist

CATEGORY	BUDGET	ACTUAL COST	DEPOSIT	BALANCE

Wedding Contact List

IMPORTANT VENDOR CONTACTS

	NAME	PHONE #	EMAIL	ADDRESS
OFFICIANT				
RECEPTION VENUE				
WEDDING SHOP				
TAILOR				
FLORIST				
CATERER				
DJ/ENTERTAINMENT				
WEDDING VENUE				
TRANSPORTATION				
OTHER:				
OTHER:				
OTHER:				

NOTES & More

SPECIAL REMINDERS

Planning Snapshot

CEREMONY EXPENSE TRACKER

	BUDGET	COST	DEPOSIT	BALANCE	DUE DATE
OFFICIANT GRATUITY					
MARRIAGE LICENSE					
VENUE COST					
FLOWERS					
DECORATIONS					
OTHER					

NOTES & Reminders

NOTES & REMINDERS

RECEPTION EXPENSE TRACKER

	BUDGET	COST	DEPOSIT	BALANCE	DUE DATE
VENUE FEE					
CATERING/FOOD					
BAR/BEVERAGES					
CAKE/CUTTING FEE					
DECORATIONS					
RENTALS/EXTRAS					
BARTENDER/STAFF					

NOTES & More

SPECIAL REMINDERS

Planning Snapshot

PAPER PRODUCTS EXPENSE TRACKER

	BUDGET	COST	DEPOSIT	BALANCE	DUE DATE
INVITATIONS/CARDS					
POSTAGE COSTS					
THANK YOU CARDS					
PLACE CARDS					
GUESTBOOK					
OTHER					

NOTES & Reminders

NOTES & REMINDERS

ENTERTAINMENT EXPENSE TRACKER

	BUDGET	COST	DEPOSIT	BALANCE	DUE DATE
BAND/DJ					
SOUND SYSTEM RENTAL					
VENUE/DANCE RENTAL					
GRATUITIES					
OTHER:					
OTHER:					
OTHER:					

NOTES & More

SPECIAL REMINDERS

Planning Snapshot

WEDDING PARTY ATTIRE EXPENSE TRACKER

	BUDGET	COST	DEPOSIT	BALANCE	DUE DATE
TUX RENTALS					
BRIDESMAN SUIT					
SHOES					
VEIL/GARTER/OTHER					
ALTERATION COSTS					

NOTES & Reminders

NOTES & REMINDERS

TRANSPORTATION EXPENSE TRACKER

	BUDGET	COST	DEPOSIT	BALANCE	DUE DATE
LIMO RENTAL					
VALET PARKING					
VENUE TRANSPORTATION					
AIRPORT TRANSPORTATION					
OTHER:					
OTHER:					
OTHER:					

NOTES & More

SPECIAL REMINDERS

Planning Snapshot

FLORIST EXPENSE TRACKER

	BUDGET	COST	DEPOSIT	BALANCE	DUE DATE
VENUE DECORATIONS					
BOUTONNIERES					
VASES/EXTRAS					
TABLE DECORATIONS					
OTHER:					

NOTES & Reminders

NOTES & REMINDERS

OTHER EXPENSE TRACKER

	BUDGET	COST	DEPOSIT	BALANCE	DUE DATE
PHOTOGRAPHER					
VIDEOGRAPHER					
CATERER					
HAIR/SALON					
WEDDING RINGS					
WEDDING PARTY GIFTS					
OTHER:					

NOTES & More

SPECIAL REMINDERS

Groom's Planner

HAIR APPOINTMENT

SALON NAME	DATE	TIME	BOOKED FOR:		ADDRESS:
			☐		
			☐		
			☐		

NOTES

TUX FITTING APPOINTMENT

BUSINESS NAME	DATE	TIME	BOOKED FOR:		ADDRESS:
			☐		
			☐		

NOTES

OTHER:

BUSINESS NAME	DATE	TIME	BOOKED FOR:		ADDRESS:
			☐		
			☐		
			☐		

NOTES

Important Dates

DATE:	DATE:	DATE:	REMINDERS
DATE:	DATE:	DATE:	
DATE:	DATE:	DATE:	
			NOTES
DATE:	DATE:	DATE:	
DATE:	DATE:	DATE:	

Weekly Wedding Planning

WEEK OF: _____

MONDAY

TUESDAY

WEDNESDAY

THURSDAY

FRIDAY

SATURDAY

WEDDING TO DO LIST

☐ _____
☐ _____
☐ _____
☐ _____
☐ _____
☐ _____
☐ _____
☐ _____
☐ _____
☐ _____
☐ _____
☐ _____
☐ _____
☐ _____
☐ _____
☐ _____

APPOINTMENTS & MEETINGS

DATE	TIME	VENDOR	PURPOSE

Weekly Wedding Planning

WEEK OF: _____

MONDAY

WEDDING TO DO LIST

- [ ] _____
- [ ] _____
- [ ] _____
- [ ] _____
- [ ] _____
- [ ] _____
- [ ] _____
- [ ] _____
- [ ] _____
- [ ] _____
- [ ] _____
- [ ] _____
- [ ] _____
- [ ] _____
- [ ] _____
- [ ] _____

TUESDAY

WEDNESDAY

THURSDAY

APPOINTMENTS & MEETINGS

DATE	TIME	VENDOR	PURPOSE

FRIDAY

SATURDAY

Weekly Wedding Planning

WEEK OF: _____

MONDAY

TUESDAY

WEDNESDAY

THURSDAY

FRIDAY

SATURDAY

WEDDING TO DO LIST

☐ _____
☐ _____
☐ _____
☐ _____
☐ _____
☐ _____
☐ _____
☐ _____
☐ _____
☐ _____
☐ _____
☐ _____
☐ _____
☐ _____
☐ _____
☐ _____
☐ _____

APPOINTMENTS & MEETINGS

DATE	TIME	VENDOR	PURPOSE

Weekly Wedding Planning

WEEK OF: _____

MONDAY

TUESDAY

WEDNESDAY

THURSDAY

FRIDAY

SATURDAY

WEDDING TO DO LIST

- [ ] _____
- [ ] _____
- [ ] _____
- [ ] _____
- [ ] _____
- [ ] _____
- [ ] _____
- [ ] _____
- [ ] _____
- [ ] _____
- [ ] _____
- [ ] _____
- [ ] _____
- [ ] _____
- [ ] _____
- [ ] _____
- [ ] _____

APPOINTMENTS & MEETINGS			
DATE	TIME	VENDOR	PURPOSE

Weekly Wedding Planning

WEEK OF: _____

MONDAY

WEDDING TO DO LIST

- [ ] _____
- [ ] _____
- [ ] _____
- [ ] _____
- [ ] _____
- [ ] _____
- [ ] _____
- [ ] _____
- [ ] _____
- [ ] _____
- [ ] _____
- [ ] _____
- [ ] _____
- [ ] _____
- [ ] _____
- [ ] _____

TUESDAY

WEDNESDAY

THURSDAY

APPOINTMENTS & MEETINGS			
DATE	TIME	VENDOR	PURPOSE

FRIDAY

SATURDAY

Weekly Wedding Planning

WEEK OF: _____

MONDAY

TUESDAY

WEDNESDAY

THURSDAY

FRIDAY

SATURDAY

WEDDING TO DO LIST

☐ _____
☐ _____
☐ _____
☐ _____
☐ _____
☐ _____
☐ _____
☐ _____
☐ _____
☐ _____
☐ _____
☐ _____
☐ _____
☐ _____
☐ _____
☐ _____

APPOINTMENTS & MEETINGS

DATE	TIME	VENDOR	PURPOSE

Weekly Wedding Planning

WEEK OF: _____

MONDAY

WEDDING TO DO LIST
☐ _____
☐ _____
☐ _____
☐ _____
☐ _____
☐ _____
☐ _____
☐ _____
☐ _____
☐ _____
☐ _____
☐ _____
☐ _____
☐ _____

TUESDAY

WEDNESDAY

THURSDAY

FRIDAY

SATURDAY

APPOINTMENTS & MEETINGS

DATE	TIME	VENDOR	PURPOSE

Weekly Wedding Planning

WEEK OF: _____

MONDAY

TUESDAY

WEDNESDAY

THURSDAY

FRIDAY

SATURDAY

WEDDING TO DO LIST

- ☐ _____
- ☐ _____
- ☐ _____
- ☐ _____
- ☐ _____
- ☐ _____
- ☐ _____
- ☐ _____
- ☐ _____
- ☐ _____
- ☐ _____
- ☐ _____
- ☐ _____
- ☐ _____
- ☐ _____
- ☐ _____

APPOINTMENTS & MEETINGS

DATE	TIME	VENDOR	PURPOSE

Weekly Wedding Planning

WEEK OF: _____

MONDAY

TUESDAY

WEDNESDAY

THURSDAY

FRIDAY

SATURDAY

WEDDING TO DO LIST

- ☐ _____
- ☐ _____
- ☐ _____
- ☐ _____
- ☐ _____
- ☐ _____
- ☐ _____
- ☐ _____
- ☐ _____
- ☐ _____
- ☐ _____
- ☐ _____
- ☐ _____
- ☐ _____
- ☐ _____
- ☐ _____

APPOINTMENTS & MEETINGS

DATE	TIME	VENDOR	PURPOSE

Weekly Wedding Planning

WEEK OF: _____

MONDAY

WEDDING TO DO LIST

- [ ] _____
- [ ] _____
- [ ] _____
- [ ] _____
- [ ] _____
- [ ] _____
- [ ] _____
- [ ] _____
- [ ] _____
- [ ] _____
- [ ] _____
- [ ] _____
- [ ] _____
- [ ] _____
- [ ] _____
- [ ] _____

TUESDAY

WEDNESDAY

THURSDAY

APPOINTMENTS & MEETINGS			
DATE	TIME	VENDOR	PURPOSE

FRIDAY

SATURDAY

Weekly Wedding Planning

WEEK OF: _____

MONDAY

WEDDING TO DO LIST

- [ ] _____
- [ ] _____
- [ ] _____
- [ ] _____
- [ ] _____
- [ ] _____
- [ ] _____
- [ ] _____
- [ ] _____
- [ ] _____
- [ ] _____
- [ ] _____
- [ ] _____
- [ ] _____
- [ ] _____
- [ ] _____

TUESDAY

WEDNESDAY

THURSDAY

APPOINTMENTS & MEETINGS			
DATE	TIME	VENDOR	PURPOSE

FRIDAY

SATURDAY

Weekly Wedding Planning

WEEK OF: _____

MONDAY

TUESDAY

WEDNESDAY

THURSDAY

FRIDAY

SATURDAY

WEDDING TO DO LIST

- ☐ _____
- ☐ _____
- ☐ _____
- ☐ _____
- ☐ _____
- ☐ _____
- ☐ _____
- ☐ _____
- ☐ _____
- ☐ _____
- ☐ _____
- ☐ _____
- ☐ _____
- ☐ _____
- ☐ _____
- ☐ _____

APPOINTMENTS & MEETINGS			
DATE	TIME	VENDOR	PURPOSE

Weekly Wedding Planning

WEEK OF: _____

MONDAY

TUESDAY

WEDNESDAY

THURSDAY

FRIDAY

SATURDAY

WEDDING TO DO LIST

- ☐ _____
- ☐ _____
- ☐ _____
- ☐ _____
- ☐ _____
- ☐ _____
- ☐ _____
- ☐ _____
- ☐ _____
- ☐ _____
- ☐ _____
- ☐ _____
- ☐ _____
- ☐ _____
- ☐ _____

APPOINTMENTS & MEETINGS			
DATE	TIME	VENDOR	PURPOSE

Weekly Wedding Planning

WEEK OF: _____

MONDAY

TUESDAY

WEDNESDAY

THURSDAY

FRIDAY

SATURDAY

WEDDING TO DO LIST

- ☐ _____
- ☐ _____
- ☐ _____
- ☐ _____
- ☐ _____
- ☐ _____
- ☐ _____
- ☐ _____
- ☐ _____
- ☐ _____
- ☐ _____
- ☐ _____
- ☐ _____
- ☐ _____
- ☐ _____
- ☐ _____

APPOINTMENTS & MEETINGS

DATE	TIME	VENDOR	PURPOSE

Weekly Wedding Planning

WEEK OF: _____

MONDAY

WEDDING TO DO LIST

- ☐ _____
- ☐ _____
- ☐ _____
- ☐ _____
- ☐ _____
- ☐ _____
- ☐ _____
- ☐ _____
- ☐ _____
- ☐ _____
- ☐ _____
- ☐ _____
- ☐ _____
- ☐ _____
- ☐ _____
- ☐ _____
- ☐ _____

TUESDAY

WEDNESDAY

THURSDAY

APPOINTMENTS & MEETINGS

DATE	TIME	VENDOR	PURPOSE

FRIDAY

SATURDAY

Weekly Wedding Planning

WEEK OF: _____

MONDAY

TUESDAY

WEDNESDAY

THURSDAY

FRIDAY

SATURDAY

WEDDING TO DO LIST

- [ ] _____
- [ ] _____
- [ ] _____
- [ ] _____
- [ ] _____
- [ ] _____
- [ ] _____
- [ ] _____
- [ ] _____
- [ ] _____
- [ ] _____
- [ ] _____
- [ ] _____
- [ ] _____
- [ ] _____

APPOINTMENTS & MEETINGS

DATE	TIME	VENDOR	PURPOSE

Weekly Wedding Planning

WEEK OF: _____

MONDAY

TUESDAY

WEDNESDAY

THURSDAY

FRIDAY

SATURDAY

WEDDING TO DO LIST

- ☐ _____
- ☐ _____
- ☐ _____
- ☐ _____
- ☐ _____
- ☐ _____
- ☐ _____
- ☐ _____
- ☐ _____
- ☐ _____
- ☐ _____
- ☐ _____
- ☐ _____
- ☐ _____
- ☐ _____

APPOINTMENTS & MEETINGS

DATE	TIME	VENDOR	PURPOSE

Weekly Wedding Planning

WEEK OF: _____

MONDAY

TUESDAY

WEDNESDAY

THURSDAY

FRIDAY

SATURDAY

WEDDING TO DO LIST

- [ ] _____
- [ ] _____
- [ ] _____
- [ ] _____
- [ ] _____
- [ ] _____
- [ ] _____
- [ ] _____
- [ ] _____
- [ ] _____
- [ ] _____
- [ ] _____
- [ ] _____
- [ ] _____
- [ ] _____
- [ ] _____

APPOINTMENTS & MEETINGS

DATE	TIME	VENDOR	PURPOSE

Weekly Wedding Planning

WEEK OF: _____

MONDAY

TUESDAY

WEDNESDAY

THURSDAY

FRIDAY

SATURDAY

WEDDING TO DO LIST

☐ _____
☐ _____
☐ _____
☐ _____
☐ _____
☐ _____
☐ _____
☐ _____
☐ _____
☐ _____
☐ _____
☐ _____
☐ _____
☐ _____
☐ _____
☐ _____
☐ _____

APPOINTMENTS & MEETINGS

DATE	TIME	VENDOR	PURPOSE

Weekly Wedding Planning

WEEK OF: _____

MONDAY

TUESDAY

WEDNESDAY

THURSDAY

FRIDAY

SATURDAY

WEDDING TO DO LIST

- [ ] _____
- [ ] _____
- [ ] _____
- [ ] _____
- [ ] _____
- [ ] _____
- [ ] _____
- [ ] _____
- [ ] _____
- [ ] _____
- [ ] _____
- [ ] _____
- [ ] _____
- [ ] _____
- [ ] _____

APPOINTMENTS & MEETINGS

DATE	TIME	VENDOR	PURPOSE

Wedding Planner

- PLANNING GUIDELINE -

SET THE DATE	CONSIDER FLORISTS	CONSIDER MUSIC CHOICES
SET YOUR BUDGET	RESEARCH CATERERS	CONSIDER MUSIC LIST
CONSIDER WEDDING THEMES	DECIDE ON OFFICIANT	CONSIDER TRANSPORTATION
PLAN ENGAGEMENT PARTY	CREATE INITIAL GUEST LIST	CREATE INITIAL GUEST LIST
RESEARCH POSSIBLE VENUES	CHOOSE WEDDING PARTY	CHOOSE WEDDING PARTY
START RESEARCHING TUXEDOS	CONSIDER ACCESSORIES	BRIDESMAN SUIT
RESEARCH PHOTOGRAPHERS	REGISTER WITH GIFT REGISTRY	BOOK TENTATIVE HOTELS
RESEARCH VIDEOGRAPHERS	DISCUSS HONEYMOON IDEAS	CONSIDER BEAUTY SALONS
RESEARCH DJS/ENTERTAINMENT	RESEARCH WEDDING RINGS	CONSIDER SHOES & OTHER

Things To Do	Status

TOP PRIORITIES

NOTES & IDEAS

APPOINTMENTS & REMINDERS

Wedding Planner

- PLANNING GUIDELINE -

9 Months BEFORE WEDDING

FINALIZE GUEST LIST

ORDER INVITATIONS

PLAN YOUR RECEPTION

BOOK PHOTOGRAPHER

BOOK VIDEOGRAPHER

CHOOSE WEDDING TUXEDO

ORDER BRIDESMAN SUIT

RESERVE WEDDING TUXEDO

ARRANGE TRANSPORTATION

BOOK WEDDING VENUE

BOOK RECEPTION VENUE

PLAN HONEYMOON

BOOK FLORIST

BOOK DJ/ENTERTAINMENT

BOOK CATERER

CHOOSE WEDDING CAKE

BOOK OFFICIANT

BOOK ROOMS FOR GUESTS

Things To Do	Status

TOP PRIORITIES

NOTES & IDEAS

APPOINTMENTS & REMINDERS

Wedding Planner

- PLANNING GUIDELINE -

6 Months BEFORE WEDDING

ORDER THANK YOU NOTES

REVIEW RECEPTION DETAILS

MAKE APPT FOR FITTING

CONFIRM TUXEDOS

OBTAIN MARRIAGE LICENSE

BOOK HAIR STYLIST

CONFIRM MUSIC SELECTION

WRITE VOWS

PLAN REHEARSAL

BOOK REHEARSAL DINNER

CONFIRM HOTEL ROOMS

SHOP FOR WEDDING RINGS

PLAN DECORATIONS

CHOOSE BOUTONNIERES TYPE

FINALIZE GUEST LIST

UPDATE PASSPORTS

Things To Do	Status

TOP PRIORITIES

NOTES & IDEAS

APPOINTMENTS & REMINDERS

Wedding Planner

- PLANNING GUIDELINE -

MAIL OUT INVITATIONS	FINALIZE HONEYMOON PLANS	CONFIRM CATERER
MEET WITH OFFICIANT	ATTEND FIRST TUXEDO FITTING	FINALIZE RING FITTING
BUY WEDDING FAVORS	FINALIZE VOWS	CONFIRM FLOWERS
BUY WEDDING PARTY GIFTS	FINALIZE RECEPTION MENU	CONFIRM BAND
PURCHASE SHOES	KEEP TRACK OF RSVPS	SHOP FOR HONEYMOON
FINALIZE THANK YOU CARDS	BOOK PHOTO SESSION	

Things To Do   Status

TOP PRIORITIES

NOTES & IDEAS

APPOINTMENTS & REMINDERS

Wedding Planner

- PLANNING GUIDELINE -

CHOOSE YOUR MC

REQUEST SPECIAL TOASTS

ARRANGE TRANSPORTATION

CHOOSE YOUR HAIR STYLE

FINALIZE WEDDING DUTIES

CREATE WEDDING SCHEDULE

CONFIRM CAKE CHOICES

CONFIRM MENU (FINAL)

CONFIRM SEATING

CONFIRM VIDEOGRAPHER

ARRANGE LEGAL DOCS

CONFIRM BRIDESMAN SUIT

MEET WITH DJ/MC

FINAL TUXEDO FITTING

WRAP WEDDIING PARTY GIFTS

CONFIRM FINAL GUEST COUNT

Things To Do

Status

TOP PRIORITIES

NOTES & IDEAS

APPOINTMENTS & REMINDERS

Wedding Planner

- PLANNING GUIDELINE -

PAYMENT TO VENDORS

PACK FOR HONEYMOON

PICK UP TUXEDO

CONFIRM RINGS FIT

CONFIRM HOTEL RESERVATION

GIVE MUSIC LIST TO DJ/BAND

CONFIRM TRAVEL PLANS

GIVE SCHEDULE TO PARTY

CONFIRM SHOES FIT

CONFIRM HOTELS FOR GUESTS

DELIVER LICENSE TO OFFICIANT

CONFIRM TRANSPORTATION

OTHER: _____

CONFIRM WITH VENDORS

MONEY FOR GRATUITIES

OTHER: _____

Things To Do

Status

TOP PRIORITIES

NOTES & IDEAS

APPOINTMENTS & REMINDERS

Wedding Planner
- PLANNING GUIDELINE -

1 Day BEFORE WEDDING

ATTEND REHEARSAL DINNER

CHECK WEATHER TO PREPARE

GIVE GIFTS TO WEDDING PARTY

FINISH HONEYMOON PACKING

CHECK ON WEDDING VENUE

CONFIRM RINGS FIT

GREET OUT OF TOWN GUESTS

GET A GOOD NIGHT'S SLEEP

Things To Do

Status

TOP PRIORITIES

NOTES & IDEAS

APPOINTMENTS & REMINDERS

Your Special Day!

Day of WEDDING

GET YOUR HAIR DONE

HAVE A LIGHT BREAKFAST

GIVE RINGS TO BEST MAN

ENJOY YOUR SPECIAL DAY!

Wedding Attire Planner

WEDDING ATTIRE EXPENSE TRACKER

ITEM/PURCHASE	STATUS ✓	DATE PAID	TOTAL COST

NOTES & REMINDERS

TOTAL COST:

Notes:

WEDDING ATTIRE DETAILS

Venue Planner

VENUE EXPENSE TRACKER			
ITEM/PURCHASE	STATUS ✓	DATE PAID	TOTAL COST

NOTES & REMINDERS

TOTAL COST:

Notes:

VENUE PLANNING DETAILS

Catering Planner

CATERING EXPENSE TRACKER

ITEM/PURCHASE	STATUS ✓	DATE PAID	TOTAL COST

NOTES & REMINDERS

TOTAL COST:

Notes:

CATERING PLANNER DETAILS

Entertainment Planner

ENTERTAINMENT EXPENSE TRACKER

ITEM/PURCHASE	STATUS ✓	DATE PAID	TOTAL COST

NOTES & REMINDERS

TOTAL COST:

Notes:

ENTERTAINMENT DETAILS

Videographer Planner

VIDEOGRAPHER EXPENSE TRACKER			
ITEM/PURCHASE	STATUS ✓	DATE PAID	TOTAL COST

NOTES & REMINDERS

TOTAL COST:

Notes:

VIDEOGRAPHER DETAILS

Photographer Planner

PHOTOGRAPHER EXPENSE TRACKER

ITEM/PURCHASE	STATUS ✓	DATE PAID	TOTAL COST

NOTES & REMINDERS

TOTAL COST:

Notes:

PHOTOGRAPHER DETAILS

Florist Planner

FLORIST EXPENSE TRACKER			
ITEM/PURCHASE	STATUS ✓	DATE PAID	TOTAL COST

NOTES & REMINDERS

TOTAL COST:

Notes:

FLORIST PLANNING DETAILS

Extra Wedding Costs

MISC WEDDING EXPENSE TRACKER			
ITEM/PURCHASE	STATUS ✓	DATE PAID	TOTAL COST

NOTES & REMINDERS

TOTAL COST:

Notes:

MISC WEDDING DETAILS

Bachelor Party Planner

EVENT DETAILS

DATE

TIME

VENUE

THEME

HOST

OTHER

TIME	SCHEDULE OF EVENTS

GUEST LIST

FIRST NAME	LAST NAME	R

SUPPLIES & SHOPPING LIST

- ☐
- ☐
- ☐
- ☐
- ☐
- ☐
- ☐
- ☐
- ☐
- ☐
- ☐
- ☐
- ☐
- ☐
- ☐

NOTES & REMINDERS

love

Reception Planner

MEAL PLANNER IDEAS

HORS D'OEUVRES

1st COURSE:

3rd COURSE:

2nd COURSE:

4th COURSE:

MEAL PLANNING NOTES

Wedding Planning Notes

IDEAS & REMINDERS

Wedding to do List

Wedding Guest List

NAME	ADDRESS	PHONE #	# IN PARTY	RSVP: ✓

Wedding Guest List

NAME	ADDRESS	PHONE #	# IN PARTY	RSVP: ✓

Wedding Guest List

NAME	ADDRESS	PHONE #	# IN PARTY	RSVP: ✓

Wedding Guest List

NAME	ADDRESS	PHONE #	# IN PARTY	RSVP: ✓

Wedding Guest List

NAME	ADDRESS	PHONE #	# IN PARTY	RSVP: ✓

Wedding Guest List

NAME	ADDRESS	PHONE #	# IN PARTY	RSVP: ✓

Wedding Guest List

NAME	ADDRESS	PHONE #	# IN PARTY	RSVP: ✓

Wedding Guest List

NAME	ADDRESS	PHONE #	# IN PARTY	RSVP: ✓

Wedding Guest List

NAME	ADDRESS	PHONE #	# IN PARTY	RSVP: ✓

Wedding Guest List

NAME	ADDRESS	PHONE #	# IN PARTY	RSVP: ✓

Wedding Guest List

NAME	ADDRESS	PHONE #	# IN PARTY	RSVP: ✓

Wedding Guest List

NAME	ADDRESS	PHONE #	# IN PARTY	RSVP: ✓

Wedding Seating Chart

Table #

TABLE #:

1:

2:

3:

4:

5:

6:

7:

8:

Table #

TABLE #:

1:

2:

3:

4:

5:

6:

7:

8:

Wedding Seating Chart

Table #

Table #

TABLE #:

1:

2:

3:

4:

5:

6:

7:

8:

TABLE #:

1:

2:

3:

4:

5:

6:

7:

8:

Wedding Seating Chart

Table #

TABLE #:

1:

2:

3:

4:

5:

6:

7:

8:

Table #

TABLE #:

1:

2:

3:

4:

5:

6:

7:

8:

Wedding Seating Chart

Table #

TABLE #:
1 :
2 :
3 :
4 :
5 :
6 :
7 :
8 :

Table #

TABLE #:
1 :
2 :
3 :
4 :
5 :
6 :
7 :
8 :

Wedding Seating Chart

Table #

TABLE #:
1 :
2 :
3 :
4 :
5 :
6 :
7 :
8 :

Table #

TABLE #:
1 :
2 :
3 :
4 :
5 :
6 :
7 :
8 :

Wedding Seating Chart

Table #

TABLE #:

1:

2:

3:

4:

5:

6:

7:

8:

Table #

TABLE #:

1:

2:

3:

4:

5:

6:

7:

8:

Wedding Seating Chart

Table #

TABLE #:

1:

2:

3:

4:

5:

6:

7:

8:

Table #

TABLE #:

1:

2:

3:

4:

5:

6:

7:

8:

Wedding Seating Chart

Table #

TABLE #:

1 :

2 :

3 :

4 :

5 :

6 :

7 :

8 :

Table #

TABLE #:

1 :

2 :

3 :

4 :

5 :

6 :

7 :

8 :

Wedding Seating Chart

Table #

TABLE #:

1:

2:

3:

4:

5:

6:

7:

8:

Table #

TABLE #:

1:

2:

3:

4:

5:

6:

7:

8:

Wedding Seating Chart

Table #

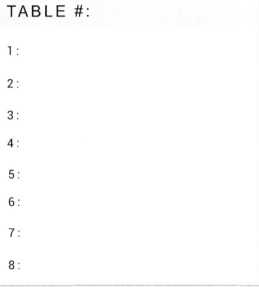

TABLE #:

1 :

2 :

3 :

4 :

5 :

6 :

7 :

8 :

Table #

TABLE #:

1 :

2 :

3 :

4 :

5 :

6 :

7 :

8 :

Wedding Seating Chart

Table #

TABLE #:
1 :
2 :
3 :
4 :
5 :
6 :
7 :
8 :

Table #

TABLE #:
1 :
2 :
3 :
4 :
5 :
6 :
7 :
8 :

Wedding Seating Chart

Table #

TABLE #:

1 :

2 :

3 :

4 :

5 :

6 :

7 :

8 :

Table #

TABLE #:

1 :

2 :

3 :

4 :

5 :

6 :

7 :

8 :

Wedding Seating Chart

Table #

TABLE #:
1 :
2 :
3 :
4 :
5 :
6 :
7 :
8 :

Table #

TABLE #:
1 :
2 :
3 :
4 :
5 :
6 :
7 :
8 :

Wedding Seating Chart

Table #

TABLE #:

1:

2:

3:

4:

5:

6:

7:

8:

Table #

TABLE #:

1:

2:

3:

4:

5:

6:

7:

8:

Wedding Seating Chart

Table #

TABLE #:
1 :
2 :
3 :
4 :
5 :
6 :
7 :
8 :

Table #

TABLE #:
1 :
2 :
3 :
4 :
5 :
6 :
7 :
8 :

Wedding Seating Chart

Table #

TABLE #:
1 :
2 :
3 :
4 :
5 :
6 :
7 :
8 :

Table #

TABLE #:
1 :
2 :
3 :
4 :
5 :
6 :
7 :
8 :

Wedding Seating Chart

Table #

TABLE #:

1 :

2 :

3 :

4 :

5 :

6 :

7 :

8 :

Table #

TABLE #:

1 :

2 :

3 :

4 :

5 :

6 :

7 :

8 :

Wedding Seating Chart

Table #

TABLE #:
1 :
2 :
3 :
4 :
5 :
6 :
7 :
8 :

Table #

TABLE #:
1 :
2 :
3 :
4 :
5 :
6 :
7 :
8 :

Wedding Seating Chart

Table #

TABLE #:
1 :
2 :
3 :
4 :
5 :
6 :
7 :
8 :

Table #

TABLE #:
1 :
2 :
3 :
4 :
5 :
6 :
7 :
8 :

Wedding Seating Chart

Table #

TABLE #:
1 :
2 :
3 :
4 :
5 :
6 :
7 :
8 :

Table #

TABLE #:
1 :
2 :
3 :
4 :
5 :
6 :
7 :
8 :

Wedding Seating Chart

Table #

TABLE #:

1:

2:

3:

4:

5:

6:

7:

8:

Table #

TABLE #:

1:

2:

3:

4:

5:

6:

7:

8:

Wedding Seating Chart

Table #

TABLE #:

1:

2:

3:

4:

5:

6:

7:

8:

Table #

TABLE #:

1:

2:

3:

4:

5:

6:

7:

8:

Wedding Seating Chart

Table #

TABLE #:

1:

2:

3:

4:

5:

6:

7:

8:

Table #

TABLE #:

1:

2:

3:

4:

5:

6:

7:

8:

Wedding Seating Chart

Table #

TABLE #:

1:

2:

3:

4:

5:

6:

7:

8:

Table #

TABLE #:

1:

2:

3:

4:

5:

6:

7:

8:

Wedding Seating Chart

Table #

TABLE #:

1 :

2 :

3 :

4 :

5 :

6 :

7 :

8 :

Table #

TABLE #:

1 :

2 :

3 :

4 :

5 :

6 :

7 :

8 :

Wedding Seating Chart

Table #

TABLE #:

1 :

2 :

3 :

4 :

5 :

6 :

7 :

8 :

Table #

TABLE #:

1 :

2 :

3 :

4 :

5 :

6 :

7 :

8 :

Wedding Seating Chart

Table #

TABLE #:

1:	2:	3:	4:	5:	6:	7:	8:
9:	10:	11:	12:	13:	14:	15:	16:

Table #

TABLE #:

1:	2:	3:	4:	5:	6:	7:	8:
9:	10:	11:	12:	13:	14:	15:	16:

Wedding Seating Chart

Table #

TABLE #:

1:	2:	3:	4:	5:	6:	7:	8:
9:	10:	11:	12:	13:	14:	15:	16:

Table #

TABLE #:

1:	2:	3:	4:	5:	6:	7:	8:
9:	10:	11:	12:	13:	14:	15:	16:

Wedding Seating Chart

Table #

TABLE #:

1:	2:	3:	4:	5:	6:	7:	8:
9:	10:	11:	12:	13:	14:	15:	16:

Table #

TABLE #:

1:	2:	3:	4:	5:	6:	7:	8:
9:	10:	11:	12:	13:	14:	15:	16:

Wedding Seating Chart

Table #

TABLE #:

1:	2:	3:	4:	5:	6:	7:	8:
9:	10:	11:	12:	13:	14:	15:	16:

Table #

TABLE #:

1:	2:	3:	4:	5:	6:	7:	8:
9:	10:	11:	12:	13:	14:	15:	16:

Wedding Seating Chart

Table #

TABLE #:

1:	2:	3:	4:	5:	6:	7:	8:
9:	10:	11:	12:	13:	14:	15:	16:

Table #

TABLE #:

1:	2:	3:	4:	5:	6:	7:	8:
9:	10:	11:	12:	13:	14:	15:	16:

Wedding Seating Chart

Table #

TABLE #:

1:	2:	3:	4:	5:	6:	7:	8:
9:	10:	11:	12:	13:	14:	15:	16:

Table #

TABLE #:

1:	2:	3:	4:	5:	6:	7:	8:
9:	10:	11:	12:	13:	14:	15:	16:

Wedding Seating Chart

Table #

TABLE #:

1:	2:	3:	4:	5:	6:	7:	8:
9:	10:	11:	12:	13:	14:	15:	16:

Table #

TABLE #:

1:	2:	3:	4:	5:	6:	7:	8:
9:	10:	11:	12:	13:	14:	15:	16:

Wedding Seating Chart

Table #

TABLE #:

1:	2:	3:	4:	5:	6:	7:	8:
9:	10:	11:	12:	13:	14:	15:	16:

Table #

TABLE #:

1:	2:	3:	4:	5:	6:	7:	8:
9:	10:	11:	12:	13:	14:	15:	16:

Wedding Seating Chart

Table #

TABLE #:

1:	2:	3:	4:	5:	6:	7:	8:
9:	10:	11:	12:	13:	14:	15:	16:

Table #

TABLE #:

1:	2:	3:	4:	5:	6:	7:	8:
9:	10:	11:	12:	13:	14:	15:	16:

Wedding Seating Chart

Table #

TABLE #:

1:	2:	3:	4:	5:	6:	7:	8:
9:	10:	11:	12:	13:	14:	15:	16:

Table #

TABLE #:

1:	2:	3:	4:	5:	6:	7:	8:
9:	10:	11:	12:	13:	14:	15:	16:

Wedding Seating Chart

Table #

TABLE #:

1:	2:	3:	4:	5:	6:	7:	8:
9:	10:	11:	12:	13:	14:	15:	16:

Table #

TABLE #:

1:	2:	3:	4:	5:	6:	7:	8:
9:	10:	11:	12:	13:	14:	15:	16:

Made in the USA
Middletown, DE
09 October 2022